MY FRIEND WITH AUTISM

by Elizabeth Andrews

Cody Koala

An Imprint of Pop!

popbooksonline.com

Hello! My name is Cody Koala

This book is filled with videos, puzzles, games, and more! Scan the QR codes* while you read, or visit the website below to make this book pop.

popbooksonline.com/autism

*Scanning QR codes requires a web-enabled smart device with a QR code reader app and a camera.

abdobooks.com

Published by Pop!, a division of ABDO, PO Box 398166, Minneapolis, Minnesota 55439. Copyright ©2024 by Abdo Consulting Group, Inc. International copyrights reserved in all countries. No part of this book may be reproduced in any form without written permission from the publisher. Cody Koala™ is a trademark and logo of Pop!.

Printed in the United States of America, North Mankato, Minnesota.

102023
012024

THIS BOOK CONTAINS RECYCLED MATERIALS

Cover Photo: Shutterstock Images
Interior Photos: Shutterstock Images; Getty Images
Editor: Grace Hansen
Series Designer: Victoria Bates

Library of Congress Control Number: 2023938824

Publisher's Cataloging-in-Publication Data
Names: Andrews, Elizabeth, author.
Title: My friend with autism / by Elizabeth Andrews
Description: Minneapolis, Minnesota : Pop!, 2024 | Series: My friend with health needs | Includes online resources and index
Identifiers: ISBN 9781098245306 (lib. bdg.) | ISBN 9781098245863 (ebook)
Subjects: LCSH: Friendship--Juvenile literature. | Autism spectrum disorders--Juvenile literature. | Autistic people--Juvenile literature. | Social acceptance--Juvenile literature.
Classification: DDC 618.928588--dc23

Table of Contents

Chapter 1

Morning Routine

Mia's dad wakes her up at 7:15 a.m. After using the restroom, Mia washes her hands and face. Then, she brushes her teeth. Mia has yogurt and berries for breakfast. She follows this **routine** every morning.

Watch a video here!

Mia has autism. Autism affects the way the brain works. It causes people to do certain things and act certain ways. Following the same routine is comforting for many people with autism.

About one in 36 children in the United States is **diagnosed** with autism spectrum disorder.

Chapter 2

Autism Spectrum Disorder

Autism is a spectrum **disorder**. This means people with autism have different **symptoms**. Most people with autism are **diagnosed** before the age of five. Doctors look for signs during checkups.

Learn more here!

Autism in Boys

- Choose to be alone in social settings
- Visible **repetitive** behaviors
- Lose control of emotions in public

Autism in Girls

- Change behavior to fit into social settings
- Invisible repetitive behaviors
- Lose control of emotions at home

Many kids with autism have a hard time talking to others. Some may not speak at all. They might not make eye contact. Boys and girls often show symptoms differently.

Children with autism
often show repetitive
behaviors. These can
include body rocking and

hand flapping. Lining up
toys and making loud
noises are other examples
of repetitive behaviors.

Chapter 3

Autism in School

School can be **overwhelming** for kids with autism. In busy hallways and loud lunchrooms, a student might wear ear plugs and hold onto **sensory objects**.

School often follows the same **routine** daily. Teachers help students with autism prepare if there's ever a change in routine.

Explore links here!

Children with autism often spend time on their own. They can easily **focus** on their favorite subjects. Classmates can be kind by talking about those subjects with their friends with autism.

Chapter 4

Friends with Autism

Kids with autism often have a hard time understanding how other people feel. If your friend says something unkind, they might not know it. You can tell them nicely if they've hurt your feelings.

Complete an
activity here!

As you get to know a friend who has autism, it is important to be **patient** and kind. Friendship is as special to someone with autism as it is to anyone else.

> If you see someone being mean to your friend with health needs, tell an adult. It's good to stand up to bullying.

Making Connections

Text-to-Self

Do you have any friends who have autism? If so, what is your favorite thing to do together?

Text-to-Text

Have you read any books about other kinds of health needs? If so, how were they similar to or different from having autism?

Text-to-World

Many people with autism spectrum disorder have changed the world, including Albert Einstein. With an adult, look up more information about a person with autism who interests you. How did that person make the world a better place?

Glossary

diagnose – to recognize something, such as a disease, by signs, symptoms, or tests.

disorder – a physical or mental sickness or condition.

focus – to give attention or efforts to one thing.

overwhelming – tending to load or burden with too much of something.

patient – able to wait without complaining or becoming upset.

repetitive – involving doing or saying the same thing several times.

routine – a regular course of action that doesn't change.

sensory object – a toy designed to engage a child's senses and keep them calm.

symptom – a noticeable change in the normal working of the body.

Index

Online Resources

popbooksonline.com

Thanks for reading this Cody Koala book!

This book is filled with videos, puzzles, games, and more! Scan the QR codes* while you read, or visit the website below to make this book pop.

popbooksonline.com/autism

*Scanning QR codes requires a web-enabled smart device with a QR code reader app and a camera.